CEREBRAL CONFETTI

I0556557

Poetry and Ponderings on Travels,
Family, Sports, Loss, Faith, Love and Being Human

Eileen C Anderson

ISBN: 978-1-63103-040-6

With love and gratitude to

~ my supportive super hero husband Eric

~ my exceptional children, Jeff, Shawn and Kelly,
who have blessed my life with six brilliant grandkids

In remembrance of...

~ Sean Bunn, beloved TRSN Guvnah, Red Sox fan extraordinaire, cherished friend, loving son, proud dad and grandpa, humanitarian, phenomenal fund raiser, baseball historian, fearless giver, cancer warrior, enterprising leader, fun loving pal to all, compassionate advocate

~ Paul McClain, devoted family man, wicked witty endearing friend, gallingly steadfast Yankees fan (loved you regardless), cancer fighter, sports aficionado, inquisitive traveler, prankster, expert craftsman, nature and music lover, Renaissance man, ardent adventurer

...your hearts still smile upon us from green fields above

TABLE OF CONTENTS

PROLOGUE

So often I hear people moan over any effort which involves writing. For many, it's complete drudge, often accompanied by a loathsome attitude toward reading. Poetry often holds a particular disdain. I'll have a tough time convincing that lot to buy my book.

Both of my parents read to me, fostering an urgency to comprehend these mysterious words they articulated. Ultimately, I was polishing off primers, reading to my kindergarten class at age 4. Proudly, my daughter later did the same.

Paralleling my reading zest, I became enthralled with printing the alphabet and began writing as a youngster. In school, I was the word weirdo who relished book reports and spelling bees. Collaborating with a schoolmate, we wrote two plays in elementary school; our Christmas story was actually performed. At home, I kept diaries detailing neighborhood antics with friends, prattling on about sports, book and concert reviews, adolescent angst. I'd long been a visitor to our local public library, where giant "Reading Is Adventurous!" posters hung. I found my first job there, re-shelving books and gluing broken spines. Exploring fresh genres such as Sci Fi and poetry provided new concepts for writing topics. I'd often present my groundbreaking bon mots to mom and her friends gathered at the kitchen table, a most gracious audience. The occasional high ball likely sparked enthusiasm.

Adulthood came with increased commitments and fewer creative outlets. Time was sparse to chronicle random thoughts. Eventually, with stacks of half-finished journals and scraps of mental floss spilling out of my night stand, I reached a break point, purposely committing myself to construct some sense of order.

What follows is that garden of thought, years of inspiration from a swarm of sources, most notably my cherished family. As the title *Cerebral Confetti* implies, it's a collection of essays and poetic reflections, drafted over decades. My Canadian born mother was the catalyst for several pieces. Mumsy and I shared countless sweet memories, from intimate to pure fun, mirrored in *Un jour avec mon petit chou*. Another, *Ma Joie de Vivre*, recounts her living history. Who better than our loved ones to animate our story telling?

The photographs are originals shot at various times, mostly while traveling. The "Dinosaur" drawing was etched by my artistic daughter, Kelly. My goal is for each to complement and embellish its accompanying verse.

Adventures come in many forms. May this literary exploit be one.

Eileen Anderson
Raleigh NC

By Kelly, 2018

NOTES FROM A DANCING DINOSAUR

When I'm asked what I do for a living, my reply typically meets with beaming, engaging comments such as "I've always wanted to do that!" or sunny destination queries. As the travel industry morphed into the current plethora of web-based booking channels, remarks often skew toward how anyone could do the same thing online and who would pay fees *for that*? At one time, I was stumped. Defensive. Almost apologetic. Ask me now and pull up a chair...

I am a treasurer. I process over 1.5 million consumer dollars annually which I manage with efficiency and discretion. I am an advocate. When clients are treated unfairly or disgruntled about a service rendered, I use every tool in my arsenal to facilitate an equitable resolution. I am a counselor. I'm among the first to hear of a family death or sudden mishap causing plans to change, handling such disruptions with minimal financial and emotional impact. I am a geography geek. I study maps, memorize third world city codes and capitals, schooling myself on regions and their adjoining countries. I am a newshound. I routinely consult multiple websites (cheers! BBC, bastion of journalism) to remain informed of geopolitical events which may compromise safety or cause client distress. What other vocation encompasses such diverse skills? I am your professional Travel Advisor / Group Coordinator/ International Specialist. It's right there on my card.

I am comically reminded of being bio-designed for this career: I was a juvenile gypsy. Early expeditions involved jumping fences and straying into homes of neighbors I barely knew – as a 3 year old toddler. I grew up riding trains between Boston and New York. Dad worked for the railroad; I often tagged along. My hometown Providence Union Station is etched in memory: roughhewn entry doors, aged sky high ceilings, bustling Pullman Porters, smoky newsstands. I can still hear the thunder of arriving trains, their ear splitting rumble overhead while navigating the underground tunnels to reach the tracks, sweaty walls plastered with peeling Broadway posters. Though the whiff of diesel became routine, I was thrilled with the prospect of each trip, watching distant places roll by, face pressed to the glass. With that began a recurrent teaching moment: a gigantic world beckoned outside my window.

Fast forward a few years, my coaster bike transported me to other zones beyond my own, soaring across city lines, under bridges and freeways, past shipyards, through downtown. I'd follow city buses, losing one, I'd pick up another. Before the ink was dry on my driver's license, I'd independently driven throughout New England, to St. Louis and Canada. At age 25, I landed a Reservations job in Dallas with Braniff Airlines, taking the "company jet" to the continents of my dreams, meeting diverse, enthralling people, falling in love with their countries, food, customs, making new friends I'd keep for life. I was hooked.

With the demise of Braniff and my airline career, I migrated to new terrain, becoming a neophyte travel agent for a DC area mega agency, three blocks from the White House. It was a baptism by fire, mastering a new booking system, dealing with vacation suppliers, handling cash, tracking payments while frantically managing time strapped clients. We often had lines out the door during lunch hour. I was thoroughly overwhelmed but adapted quickly. Such a personality potpourri! The Saville Row multinationals from World Bank and IMF, type A brokers, K Street lawyers, introverted policy wonks, desk pounding government egotists, all far better informed than me. When knowledge failed, I finessed my way through.

My ever increasing skillset ordained me a "floater", working various office locations between DC and Rosslyn, becoming proficient in leisure, corporate and government travel. Though my resume was expanding, those early years were economically tough, circa the mid 1980s. As cheerful front line agency ambassadors, we were barely paid a living wage with a paltry 1 – 2 weeks of vacation and personal time inclusive. With some penny-pinching owners, long hours netted no overtime pay, such travel trolls were we. Credentials such as Certified Travel Consultant or Assistant (CTC, CTA) were still in their neonatal professional stage and had no bearing on compensation. None of us could envision the jetstream of change approaching.

During that golden age of airline commissions, we were offered more gratis airline tickets and trips than we could possibly use. By the mid 90's, those commissions were effectively abolished. Travel agencies were compelled to begin levying fees for issuing airline tickets, planning vacation travel, along with "back end" charges for cancellations. What began as an uncomfortable transition for agents and clients alike became a watershed moment in the travel industry – adapting to fee based services.

Then something curiously wonderful happened. Lackluster, dodgy agencies along with daydreamers who siphoned agents' time mostly drifted into oblivion. Travelers became more savvy, doing their homework before paying those fees. Worthy agents achieved the professional stature so long sought, at least those who earned their mettle. For those of us who stuck it out a few decades ~ the self-proclaimed dinosaurs ~ we finally began to earn a real living doing what we love.

Today's advisor is a multi-task specialist. Consider the nuances of price shopping multiple dates, (both online and in our booking systems) to secure the best deals, processing multiple payments amid various date and name changes, preparing electronic and/or paper documents, disclosing entry requirements for every third world country imaginable, then redoing everything upon notification of airline schedule changes (grrrrr). We coordinate seat assignments on multiple airline records (get those rows with extra oxygen masks for the kids!), request wheelchairs (follow up with airline required), order vegan/kosher/Hindu/special meals on international flights (ditto follow up), handle upgrades for premier travelers, and reassure intrepid flyers. All this while adhering to complex, fluid, and often bizarre airline rules to which we are bound and accountable, aware of obscurities or not.

Fewer travel pros are still handling airline tickets, whether individuals or groups. Why? Liability. Each ticket issued demands 100% accuracy or we invite the dreaded debit memo – an airline invoice for incorrect ticketing. Human failings are unacceptable. Maintaining onerous accounting records in mind numbing detail is a requisite task to dispute such notices - which often arrive a year after alleged infringement - while earning an average of $50 service fee per coach class ticket. Make that $48.25 (before taxes and monthly overhead costs) after that pesky 3.5% credit card processing fee. When chargebacks from credit card companies arise, we're also tasked with chasing down the client or potential fraudulent credit card abuser to avoid absorbing the chargeback. This part of the job is fraught with risk – which is why I don't ever refund service fees. That, and because work done cannot be undone.

Alas, the giveaways are all but gone. We earn our travel perks now based on productivity and supplier alliances; it's only fair. A key step to industry benefits for agents while establishing unique connections for clients is partnering with an international consortium; mine is Virtuoso.

A global community of highly accomplished, intensely knowledgeable agents, this network provides immeasurable, exclusive client perks, VIP entrée and services (online shoppers: take note). Agents have select access to educational, insightful journeys on upscale cruises and distinctive trips to provide enriched client experiences. We spend considerable time and personal resources upgrading our technical skills, expanding our professional database of trustworthy suppliers, acquiring new product training, the list goes on... all to maintain our proficiency in providing the highest level of service humanly possible. We share what we know; our clients are the direct beneficiaries of our collective expertise.

Once upon a time in commission land, travel agents had the luxury of pampering clients with time. Unless we're on a cruise together, it remains our most treasured resource. Nonetheless, we routinely develop client benefits with real world value, conducting personal follow up, all while balancing our monthly expenses (taxes, automation system, office rent, professional affiliations and subscriptions, supplies, utilities, etc.). Yet few among us seek a career change, especially after having paid our dues.

Why do I do it? Call me spoiled. Becoming an independent agent 17 plus years ago was the first step in my ladder to travel utopia. With a home office, I show up in my jammies, workout clothes, bathing suit (bound for the gym or stress busting hot tub out back), with coffee in hand and dog at my feet. Who could not love this life? It's a double edged sword. Such convenience can mean working early to late hours or catching up on weekends. Back to those perks...I've been the blissful beneficiary of invites which whisked me away to dream experiences, such as waltzing in full ball gown at the Hofburg Palace in Vienna, twirling a salsa under the stars in Havana, and swaying a merengue in San Juan. I have a date with Buenos Aires for a spicy tango. I've also had the unique delights of riding an Icelandic pony, helicopter trekking an Alaskan glacier, seeing the Big Five on safari, snorkeling all over the Caribbean and riding the luxurious Blue Train from Capetown to Pretoria.

By divine design, I was awakened to – and transformed by - travel with a purpose. Having specialized in humanitarian aid trips for over 20 years, I am richly blessed to work with a select group of outstanding, devoted servants who are simply the finest people on God's green earth. I am constantly uplifted by the compassionate work they do, using extensive vacation or personal time, sleeping in shared spaces/tents, eating mystery food, exposing themselves to a myriad of diseases and weather extremes, giving their utmost to make our world a better place. Among them are two annual surgical teams who operate in remote medical environments in Africa. I've joined them on a number of these trips to India, Africa, Guatemala, Cuba and post-Katrina Mississippi. How could I not be inspired?

Clients. Initially, I tried keeping my professional distance, preserving a carefully crafted wall between us. Nay, personal attachments! When I began getting invites to their weddings, corporate celebrations, birthday and retirement parties and being told I was part of *their* family - my resistance offensive collapsed. Personalities meshed, lives merged. Over the years, I've celebrated new births, engagements, hugged brides and grooms, driven all over the South, flown to Boston, Baltimore, Houston, Chicago and New York just to meet them. Real face time: both a valuable amenity and jointly rich experience web surfers never know. We laugh a lot. We've also pooled tears learning of disastrous health issues, shared broken hearts over the loss of a loved one (including furry friends), prayed and cried together to mitigate our distress and grief. I am considered both a travel partner and a friend. Much as I resisted, turns out, I can be both.

I am honored to get heartwarming feedback from both veteran and novice clients about the singular treatment they receive which I consider fundamental – airline waivers and favors, fare reductions, free hotel or car upgrades, deals on getaways. My fellow travel pros likewise extend comparable benefits to establish close relationships with their clientele; such is our modus operandi. We are driven to create optimal value for our clients' travel dollars, building long term alliances with a personal touch. Apart from the homemade cookies and muffins I deliver, I've provided travel related auction items to raise funds for orphaned children, clean water, earthquake and hurricane relief. I've hosted students overnight to defray hotel costs, have waived my own or absorbed airline fees for special circumstances and have personally monetized a needy client's ticket purchase. I never forget the source of any prosperity which comes my way. Mom taught me well – it is in giving that we receive. As always, Mom was right.

Shock alert: I've been paid extra (yes, more money!) because I didn't charge enough. Imagine that. My dear clients also recognize the value of time and service, whether spent resolving their complex ticket issues, organizing multi-city departures, or going out to the airport to intercede on their behalf, saving them significant dollars which they saw fit to share.

It gets better. I've been the grateful recipient of flowers, gift cards, wine, chocolates, and beautifully articulated, hand written notes and letters of gratitude. Some email me just to say hi if it's been a while between bookings; others call to strategize global trips or consult me for advice about joining the travel biz. And then there are those who tell me they can't do their jobs without me. I never forget – or give thanks for – how fortunate I am. Think I don't have the best job on the planet?

Apart from my agency website, I've never advertised nor sought any external means of expanding my business. Rather than amass a large customer database, my initial and ongoing objective is to have only as many clients as I could personally serve well. My travel enterprise was birthed on RnR (repeat and referral) business with thriving social connections. They rave about me to others who I then welcome into the fold; it's a cozy circuit. I get up smiling every day just because I'm looking forward to talking to one of these spectacular human beings whom I love and admire, with or without their verbal applause. Many have become dear friends. Of course, there are those who periodically challenge my price quotes and fees against the web – then call me for assistance after they're stuck, having used www.whatareyouthinkingbuyingatickethere.com. Bless their pointy little heads.

One might think my ego would be the size of a Dreamliner. Ahhh but then there was today... After ticketing a complex Thailand trip, an abrupt airline schedule change occurred a few weeks before departure, requiring ticket exchanges (fee free). The resolution process took over two weeks for six tickets due to language hurdles with the foreign-staffed, English challenged sales office. Upon returning, the trip leader called me to a) complain about seating (wasn't much left 45days prior to departure) then b) question my $50 fee ($48.25 before taxes/monthly overhead!) for one passenger's refund. I explained in detail the separate fees and processes for ticket issuance and refunds as disclosed (thrice, in two places) on each itinerary update sent. Having wisely purchased travel insurance for which all said fees and expenses could be claimed for a refund, she seemed content. I enthusiastically mentioned helping with their repeat trip next year. Her reply: We'll keep you in mind. *C'est la vie*.

Five (or six?) passports later, the ecstasy of new adventures endures... bliss of lift off, Zen of cotton clouds, exhilaration of touchdown, it never gets old. Exploring the unknown, revisiting favorite sites and sharing those experiences with others still sparks excitement, personally and professionally. I have a newer (faster!) bike now and still relish exploring fresh greenways and routes. These days, I call ahead. I'm over scaring the neighbors. I'm happiest when creating, planning and managing client travel experiences as well as my own, it's my jetway to joy.

So for those who dare ask if what I do truly merits the fees quoted, I ask them how often they travel and were they ever stuck on a trip and wished they'd had an ally to assist? Perhaps regretted they'd not engaged the services of a travel pro? There's always a familiar story. I just listen, then reach for my card. It's all right there.

Footnote: Retirement from airline ticket issuance joyfully came in July 2017

II

Starfish

I was a wacky mother
    with no common sense.
Inconsistent, insecure,
    overwhelmed by decisions.
I wasn't a joiner, a PTA mom,
    and couldn't live up to
        all I imagined
           a mother should be.

But I played soccer and baseball
    in the backyard
        with my children
and danced with them
    in the living room.
I served them ginger ale in champagne flutes
    when they were sick
and made them brownies before dinner
    so they'd tell me their problems.
I pantomimed poems at bedtime
    and fed them hope for breakfast.
And gave them extra spelling words
    to put into sentences
    so they'd go to college.
        And would settle for nothing less.

I chastised them too much
    and prayed to God to forgive me.
And I wasn't afraid
    to make a fool of myself
    to make them laugh.
        Still not.

I hugged them till they
    begged me to stop
and loved them when they
    told me not to.

And there is nothing in all creation
    I covet or would trade
for a single moment spent with each of them.
    Jewels of my life.
    Beats of my heart.

The backstory: On the Blue Train, South Africa   11/3/07

Leaving Capetown, I cried helplessly in darkness on the train after I wrote Starfish, hoping Kaye, my new friend and safari roommate, wouldn't hear me. I was a puddle of emotion. As I turned my head to the window, fractured light entered thru the gaps in the glass-encased blinds. Slowly, I began to recognize what it was. I woke up Kaye, fumbled for the remote to raise the blinds (it *was* the Blue Train, after all), and together we lay in awe of a celestial flare, twinkling stars blanketing every corner of the sky illuminating the South African plain, from the ground up, left to right, everywhere a star. Such a snow shower of firepower, sparkling, burning, so many I wondered how they kept from bumping into each other.
I couldn't stop smiling, going to sleep. What a Godly gift.

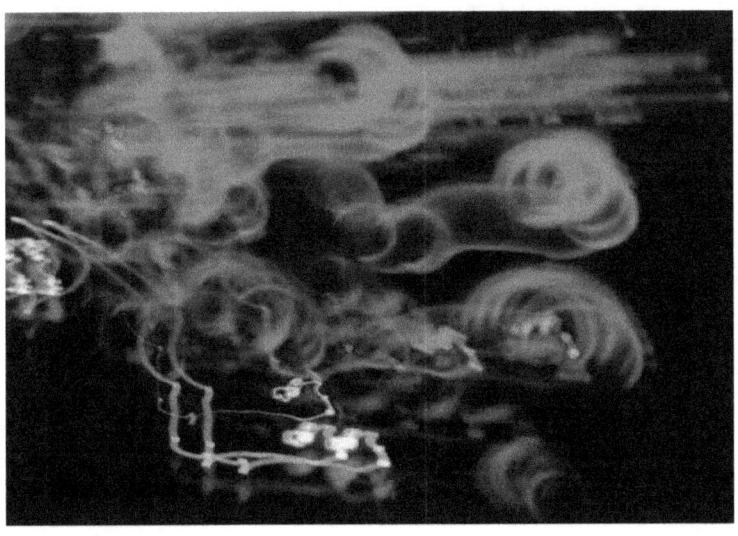

III

Of Lobster Tails and Black Travails

Tearful contrasts
    black and white
not just people
    shanty shacks
    falling down
next to shiny
    dinner plates
filled with precious food they'll never eat.
Feel so blessed to
    be on this side
    and not theirs
but still I cry
    for the sun caked mothers
    for the ragamuffin children
    for the homeless man
      laying in the gutter
      looking up at the Vuitton bag
both hoping to be boarded on the train~
    for the kind man
     who serves me
    and dreams of me
     serving him.
Still, I cry.

The backstory: On the Blue Train, South Africa 11/3/07

One could not help but notice the glaring slums along the tracks devised of random sheet metal shards, wood and industrial remnants, creating the multitude of lean-tos barely standing which served as housing for a population without privilege. It was a scene repeated town after town as our gleaming blue coaches rolled through forgotten hamlets from Capetown to Pretoria. What appeared as trash sites slowly revealed neighborhoods pock marked with trenches of filthy water, children playing in and around.

It cast a heavy pall on the riches bestowed us ~ champagne, caviar, gourmet meals, brilliantly prepared and graciously served by a squadron of wait staff (some of whom were born in this rubble), along with the finest linens in our private cars which snuggled us into cozy slumber. I've never felt so fortunate and ashamed, all at once, to witness this absurd inequality.

At one crossing, two young boys stood near the tracks to watch our magnificent marvel glide by. With impressive precision, they flipped us the bird then turned, dropped their shorts and mooned us. Some passengers near me laughed and mocked them. I wanted to be anywhere but on that train at that moment.

Still, I cry.

IV

A POLICEMAN'S PRAYER

O Lord, just for today-
Grant me one iota of Your wisdom
So I'll know when to listen and when to speak
Endow me with a trace of Your endurance
     To strengthen me until I'm off this week.

In order to effectively use my weapons
     To fight the evil forces I abhor
I ask Your holy blessing on my war toys
     That I may use my head before I draw.

Instilled within my heart's a fervent prayer
     That You'll fulfill my most sincere request
As long as I'm assured You're always there
     Most confidently, I can do my best.

Dear Lord I ask you only one thing further
     As thankfully, my tour of duty ends-
Be listening as I wake up in the morning
     Because tomorrow, I'll be on the streets again.

For Eddie and Pops, 1975

Christmas at Isaac Hunter's 2010

V

THE JOKER

I'm sarahpailin,
        parasailin'
                Through life

Don't ask me what
        Neat skills I got
Or how I came
        to stake my spot
                I'm a star

You don't have to watch
        Or even listen
As I stroke and
        game the system
             with my wand

Gone fishing in a bigger pond

I've got charm
        don't need to read
Get what support I'll ever need
        from out there
             somewhere

Can't keep me from
        a podium
I purge and gloat
        just need some notes
            or a chair

Don't have to think
        or calculate
they pay someone
        to keep me straight-
            Whazzissname?

I can't be stopped
       by reprehension
  'cause no one's even
       paying attention
             to my game

This party must be
       in some rut
'cause some think I'm
       the best they got
             Good for me!

The angry train
       that bears my name
Has just one speed
       it's all I need
           Soon I'll be

a candidate
 don't know for what
I'm spewin' style
      And kickin' butt
             Luckily...

Deep pocket friends
    write beefy checks
feed media trolls
    watch my steps
            and my foes

Newsbots suppress
      my enemies
they even face
     the facts for me
          who needs those?

Think I'm not smart?
    I don't care
just need to book my face
    out there

I feast on fear
      loathe fresh ideas
 a negation nation
       keeps me here

I quit, retreat, resurge in tweets

Why agree?
   You've got me!
We're lost in sweet ignominy
   (what'd I say?)

Go back to sleep
     real issues can keep
        can't they?

March, 2010

Cuba

VI

Adrift, aground, aloft

When I got the call
Everything stopped-
My breath,
My thoughts,
    routine distractions~

I listened,
I heard,
But didn't understand
Why you?
Why now?
Why this?

Everything in its time, He tells us~
Wait on Me, wait on Me...

I can't wait for my plants to grow
Or my nails to dry
Yet, from you, I learned to wait.

When I think of you
I think of Him
And all you taught me that He says~

He has plans
For our welfare
    not for harm
Plans to prosper us,
        for our future
He has hope. He is our hope. He is our future. He is our Father.

Behold, I make all things new, He says.

You too, will be new. Just like new.
That is my hope, my faith, my prayer.

That is what you taught me, my friend.
And that is why I love you, will love you, in this life and beyond.

To Kathy S. ~ in wellness,
                    in faith,
                            With love,
                                    Forever friends~

March 23, 2010

VII

ODE TO FENWAY

I heard some bouncing overhead
   and running all about
Jesus, hide Your sandals
   'cause Fenway's in the house

His big brown eyes looked twice their size
   when he first picked us out
Who could resist that puppy's kiss
   or knuckle-nibbling snout?

Those floppy ears outshined his peers
   with a tail wagging butt
He woofed, Hey, family, take me home!
   then he adopted us.

We primped our crib for our new kid,
bought toys galore and then bought more!

Our sixty pounds of hairy hound
   will doze right on Your lap
Cloud hopping's bound to wear him out,
   make sure he gets his naps

This perky pup will cheer You up
   when humans break Your heart
He'll sit or stay, do as You say,
   he will, he's just that smart

He'll steal your shoe - but he won't chew,
   Fen just wants to play
Chase him as he prances 'round,
   You'll get it back someday

He'll fetch Your paper, pick up sticks,
but just for treats (likes cheese and meat!)

If angel food drops on the floor
    he's quick to lick it up
Lays at Your feet, won't let You down
    Fen's a loyal pup.

We said goodbye to our furry guy
    today, with weeping hearts
We give him back to You, dear Lord
   where he first got his start.

So give him hugs from all of us
    and love him as we did
make room for frisky Fenway,
     our precious canine kid.

The backstory: We lost Fenway, our beloved 19 month old dog, on October 13th, 2010, after a series of cluster seizures. He'd had a rough start. After being found with his four siblings on a roadside near Fayetteville NC, he was taken to a rescue facility/chicken farm in Apex NC, where we met and fell in love with this adorable floppy eared puppy. He was the lone survivor in his litter; one littermate was born with no front limbs. This Yellow Lab/Vischla hybrid turned out to be a smart, alert, playful, loyal, fun loving winsome companion who never met an animal or human he didn't like (though yippy, smaller dogs scared him witless!) He vacationed with us from the beach to the mountains, visited restaurants, wineries, festivals, and hiked with us, just blended in and was welcome everywhere we went.

All dogs are special; this one was just extra special. We were a pack.

VIII

QUIZZICAL CREATURE

Who will you be ?
What color are you?
Will you heal our hearts after all we've been through?
We're happy, tearful, excited, afraid
missing the touch that brightened our day

You won't replace him, we've no expectations
you'll have surprises of your own creation

So long since the bliss of a breathy wet kiss...

Counting the days
 till this bleak winter ends
We're eager to hold you,
 to loving you, new friend

The backstory: In the weeks that followed Fenway's unexpected and painful passing, my husband Eric and I were in a deep funk. Our devoted vet, Dr. Susan Novak, was also a deeply compassionate friend and immeasurably supportive in getting us through a tough time. Though a bit sooner than expected, Susan put us on the path to finding our future canine companion. Maggie, a rescued Labradoodle, gave birth to nine pups on Thanksgiving Day, Nov 25, 2010; one fuzzy cuddlybud was soon to lift our hearts and become our new family member.

I wrote *Quizzical Creature* just before our first visit on Dec 22nd.

We fell in love, all over again.

Little Jeffrey, renamed COOPER

Cooperstown, NY   8/22/2010

IX

ETERNAL UNREST

Abner, our game is in trouble
 your children have been misbehavin'
   the booze is old hat
   they're juiced, cleats to cap
Your game is in sore want of savin'

'tis sure you'll agree with malcontent me
these boys need a slap in the head~
but since you're not here
to deliver it, dear
I'll take a swipe in your stead

Conseco's confessions are peppered with flaws
he doesn't mind telling,
defending the cause
Bonds, Sosa, McGwire –
big bucks for big bats
We buy the tickets, they taint the stats

How many juicers will sully the Hall?
How many asterisks will stink up those walls?

Tickets have outpriced a Joe's paycheck
"We earn it!" they cry, so incensed
a mere game or two
costs hundreds to view
They've plugged up the holes in the fence

Abner, we sure need your wisdom
I hear agonized cries from the grave
Is there time to get smart
 and make a fresh start
the question: can baseball be saved?

The backstory: This verse was penned sometime after the lame effort by MLB in 2003 when PED testing began. As a diehard baseball fan, I get my dander up contemplating the corrupt data created by widespread steroid use which surged in the 1990's and how long it took MLB to take action. The con artists who promoted, ignored, engaged in then lied about it exacerbate the sting. While doping is pervasive across the athletic spectrum, baseball is uniquely American and holds special rank among its diamond disciples. Stats amplified by drug use or cheating of any kind are dishonestly produced. It's unfair to the players whose excellence is overshadowed by cheaters. I'm in the camp asserting any player who used does not merit HOF* consideration. Ever.

Footnote for the uninitiated:
Legend has it that Abner Doubleday invented baseball. Grin.

*Hall Of Fame, Cooperstown NY

X

AMETHYST EYES

I'm in the world!
sang the beautiful girl
with amethyst eyes
and kodiak curls
Unfurling her magical heart-in-hand smile
Chains couldn't hold this inquisitive child

Bursting with wonder
from dusk to dawn
God's rage and mirth
its presence on earth
in this precious daughter, reborn

XI

ANGEL FACE

In every sparkling Christmas tree
My mother's face appears to me

A branch for each life lesson taught
Countless needles for good deeds wrought

Like the treetop angel, mom shines goodwill
Her heart and wisdom guide me, still

Mom taught me the simple things
that this, the happiest season brings

Giving and sharing, taking the time
to help other families with much less than mine

When I sip tea and pray for snow
Mom is doing the same, I know.

Papers are packed with holiday ads
of needless things we yearn to have

All I really need to see
is my mother's face
and a Christmas tree

Montreal, 2009

XII

Ma Joie de vivre

I was the last of four born
　　to a milliner and a mason
My mother's touch
　　was soft as chiffon,
her laughter and song, endless
　　as the spools of ribbon
　　she fashioned into graceful *chapeaux*
　　adorning the crowns of stylish women
from *savoir-faire* to *bourgeoisies*.
Her love, patient and divine.

Like the cathedral foundations he crafted,
　　my father's bones were strong and angular
His hair, a gust of charcoal smoke
　　elegantly steepled atop his weathered frame.
At day's end,
　　his arms swung wide open to receive me
　　as rough hewn doors
　　that beckon welcome
　　to prayerful patrons.

My mother's embrace
　　was a sanctuary of comfort.
My father's lap, a vestibule
　　for the tender soul
　　of a faithful child.

One brown leafless day
in a majestic *eglise*,
　　cold and lifeless,
　　with spires tolling dour knells
　　and voices chanting mournful hymns,
　　we bid *adieu* to the milliner.

Left behind was a child of compassion
  and a mason of contempt,
both without a sanctuary.

In a gesture most irreverent,
 the stone heart mason
 gave me, the child, away
to sullen sisters who claimed to be of God.
They had passion only
 for daily prayer and scolding
and knew nothing of sanctuaries of the heart.

mon pere, what did you do?
Enter sainted uncle~
who rescues me, the child,
 from a doomed adolescence
 no, a life
  of loveless discipline,
  worthless sacrifice,
  and habits most unholy.
He is my safe haven.

With life anew in a country beyond,
uncle bestows the essentials
of language, culture, customs.
In time, I bloom.

I am lifted by his lyrical spirit,
 guided by his mellow hand,
 comforted by his *serenite.*
He is selfless and divine.

The wife - another story.

A pious pity,
 ma tante zealously guards the gates
 of uncle's affection
She is a hurdle to be daily scaled.
I jump well.

Uncle and me, the girl,
we talk in the kitchen
we walk in the park
I am his blessing from a merciful God
He is my guardian angel.

One golden summer day
  in a city with rooftops
  spiraling to the heavens
Uncle takes me to a park of a different kind~
  a green cathedral
  where men play ball
  and spit tobacco.

I offer my ticket to the gatekeeper
  and recognize the chiseled hand.
I follow the road map of veins
  to the face of the stone heart mason.
Our eyes lock, hinged.

But hinges unoiled
become rusted and broken
between us, we muster
a single word spoken:
bonjour.

I walk on, the game begins.
Uncle's resolute arm surrounds me,
I close my eyes tight,
  inhale his embrace,
  reminding me of years of love
  and love given away.

I grow. I marry. I bloom again,
each new birth as precious as the first.

To my children, I give away all my gifts
  as my mother gave me~
  tenacious patience,
  warm and long embraces,
  love without measure ~
so they, too
will always know a sanctuary.

Mon pere, ma tante,
they pass.
I do not judge,
nor do I cry.

But when the saints call out
my uncle's name
watersheds of love and gratitude flow
Merci, mon oncle, merci.
I close my eyes tight and know
 he has found his eternal refuge.
Merci, Seigneur, merci.

I am now the last of four left.
The rough hewn doors open
 and beckon welcome.
I come to my *eglise* one last time
  to bid *adieu*
  to all whom I've loved
  and who loved me.
The vestibule is filled with light
 tears flow, hymns are sung.
My sanctuary *lumiere*
 burns strong and bright.

I am home.

The backstory: My mother, Jeanne, was the youngest of four daughters born to Edmond and Alphonsine Dubuc in Montreal, 1919. When her mother died, Jeanne was eight years old. Her two oldest sisters were already married; the third sister was 11 years older than Jeanne and living on her own. Why none of them were able to take her in remains a mystery. Her father then saw fit to "break up the house". He first sent her off to a convent, then onto a boarding school to be raised by nuns. She spent most of her four years there terrified of doing anything wrong that might upset one of them.

Just before finishing grade school, her Uncle Jean Dubuc, a noted sportsman and retired pro baseball player, talked his brother Edmond into allowing him to become Jeanne's guardian. He moved her to Providence, RI where she briefly attended Holy Name School, then went on to attend and graduate from Hope High School (my future alma mater).

Though a shy French speaking native, Jeanne improved her English, thrived in her new life, ever grateful for such a life changing opportunity. She was Uncle Jean's namesake and loved him dearly. He, in turn, provided her with all she needed to succeed – a comfortable home on the East Side, social introductions, language study. The only thorn in her side was his wife, Aunt Lou. Perhaps because she was childless, somewhat of a loner herself, or maybe her shoes were too tight - whatever the cause, Lou was a stern disciplinarian and rarely showed Jeanne a trace of affection. Nonetheless, Jeanne dutifully loved and greatly respected her aunt, generously describing Aunt Lou as a "second mother". However, elsewhere in her journal Jeanne relates numerous incidents that indicate otherwise.

Fortunately, Uncle Jean compensated for that abundantly. He was the essence of kindness and gentility, the way Jeanne remembered her father in the years before her mother's death. As a former Red Sox pitcher-turned-scout for the Detroit Tigers, Uncle Jean took his favorite niece to many baseball games. The incident described above actually happened: at a Red Sox home game, Aunt Lou directed Jeanne to a certain turnstile where, upon putting her ticket into the collector's hand, she recognized her father, Edmond. There he was, this once highly skilled and proud stone mason who'd built churches all over New England, reduced to being a ticket-taker at Fenway Park.*

She was stunned, as was he. They just stared at each other a few seconds, said hello, then each moved on. It was the last time she saw her father alive.

Jeanne later married and went on to bear five children of which I am one. Jeanne, my Mumsy, remains the strongest and most gentle woman I have even known. *Merci, ma mere, merci.*

Jeanne Louise Aimee Dubuc Fahey

10 MAR 1919 – 18 MAY 2008

*French Canadian stone masons were a skilled, thriving itinerant group in turn of the century

New England. Upon finishing one church or cathedral, they'd head on to the next project. Edmond worked on St. Patrick's in Providence and St. Anne's in Fall River, the site of one convent school where Jeanne was left.

Rockfish Valley, Virginia

XIII

Renewal

Do not fear for I am with you, for I am your God (Is. 41:10)

When words are not enough
to express the full measure
of what the heart wants to say
we pray for wisdom

The peace of God, which surpasses all comprehension, will guard your heart and mind (Phil.4:7)

We must allow ourselves
the gifts of patience, of time,
of dependence on others,
the anointing they share

When my spirit grows faint within me, it is You Who know my way (Ps 142:3)

Friends, loved ones,
they lift broken spirits
with selfless compassion
which blooms in us slowly

Two are better than one, if one falls down, his friend can help him up (Ecc.4:9-10)

Though our world has changed
if we can share our burdens, we will know comfort
if we can love without fear, we will know joy

Cast your cares on the Lord and He will sustain you (Ps 55:22)

If our will be strong and faith prevail
we shall know mercy
we will have peace.

For I know the plans I have for you, plans for your welfare and not for harm, plans to give you a future with hope (Jer. 29:11)

XIV

KICKING BIRTHDAY BUTT

Let's take a bus and head downtown
wearing hats, long gloves and our old prom gowns
Don our peep toe pumps and cavort in the snow
- let's just GO!

Tell the people who ask ~
Have you flipped your lids?
 we're not coco in the loco
 we're just seasoned kids!

Let's boogaloo down the dairy aisle
Shimmy shake our booty
When they laugh, we'll smile
Frolic in the fountain in our painted hose
-let's just GO!

Tell the people who ask ~
Have you flipped your lids?
 we're not coco in the loco
 we're just seasoned kids!

Let's hop a choo-choo
Just to clang the bell
Take a sky dive! Or a high dive!
Ride a five foot swell!
Boycott sittin, we ain't quittin'
 till we raise some hell!
Let's just GO!

Tell the people who ask ~
Have you flipped your lids?
 we're not coco in the loco
 we're just seasoned kids!

June 2012- July 2013

XV

....*what to say to Kelly and Ben?*

Born apart,
two different worlds
      sporting boy
      bow-dress girl

he moves North
she goes South
      both consumed with expectation, doubt

they forge ahead,
each unaware
      a loving mate is waiting there

at his intrepid door
she stands
      they glimpse their future
      hope, in hand

love erases
hurts that linger
      catch that sparkle on her finger!

born apart
brought together
      meant to share their breath forever

love embraces
blissful sight!
      when two such gifted hearts unite

May 9th, 2011
Celebrating the marriage of daughter Kelly and new son Ben on the
beach at Kitty Hawk, North Carolina, with love from Mom / Eileen

Miss. 2006

XVI

things not to do after four glashes of wine...

1. facebook high school friends
2. email high school friends with whom reunion years are measured in decades
3. invite street workers in for dinner
4. ask your sister when she's going to start dyeing her hair
5. dye your own gray hair
6. ride a bike in the dark
7. climb a privacy wall because you think you can outsmart the barking Dobermans
8. get a tattoo
9. get two tattoos
10. do inward dives off a high platform
11. remove the shower doors and light sparklers in your bathroom (unless it's a hotel room)
12. drive – anywhere
13. drive anyway, thinking a Narragansett Bay boat launch is a shortcut to Block Island
14. give your cat a perm
15. take ski lessons
16. bait a fish hook
17. eat the bait off a fish hook
18. take home an equally distressed airline passenger who just got bumped with you
19. compose a confession
20. call an old boy/girlfriend
21. write bereavement thank you notes
22. sign a real estate contract
23. sign a marriage license
24. use sign language... see where I'm going with this?

XVII

AUSTRIAN DREAM

An intrusive winter, too soon after Fall
 Frost upon frost, dire moods all~

Then came The Ball, a fairytale night
 With accessories borrowed so I'd look just right
The Ball, The Ball, champagne bubbles rule
Shrimp platters served by *garcons* uber cool

Schtrudel und schnitzel, Veltliner to drink
 my princess gown dazzled in hot lipstick pink
 The Ball, The Ball, a palatial delight
The Habsburgs insist all have fun for one night!

Snowy white debutantes, escorts sublime
 symphonic precision in one-two-three time

Bright satin epaulets, bijoux galore
Leather boots, lace heels sailing the floor
High stepping landlers, shaking the room
Oomp pa pa polkas in decorous tune

I asked him to waltz, he graciously rose,
Swept off my feet by Herr Twinkletoes
I was his Rogers; he, my Astaire
swirling the floor with circuitous flair
swooshing, stepping, changing direction
While tuxes made rounds with puffed cream cloud confections

Like magic at midnight, the ABBA songs broke!
Rock n Roll topple waltzing?
 an Ottoman choked.

Highbrows harrumphed; the bergers were fried,
Sallying forth while the beat throbbed inside

Rocking, grooving, swaying till four
Champagne bottles empty, we twirled out the door

Elatedly drained on my homeward bound flight~
Enchantment was mine for one Viennese night!

XVIII

ODE TO JOE

As the sun rises
    so goes my soul
    embraced in healing waters
    ascending heights,
    beyond earthly scale
    my faith, my vessel
    to take the place
    my Creator has saved
    for me alone.

As the sun sets
    so rests my spirit
    remaining among all whom I've loved
    and held dear
    who called me "friend".

I lived as He led me,
    lyrically inspired

to be all and only
what He desired

I leave, glowing.

For Joe Lupton, whose essence and music remains within us
(Maui) 1/14/14

XIX

KITTY

My girlish dreams
 all came to be
 in one noisy
 Irish family

What tears were shed
 mattered less
 than my family's
happiness

I loved a man
 we built a life
 cherished husband,
 hearty wife

My children thrive,
 our hopes repeat
 to rest I go,
 my dreams complete.

For Kitty Rooney, 16DEC2012, a smiling heart whose light still glows

XX

MY ONE AND ONLY

The roads in life are many
lush with handsome views
Though many pathways fascinate
I choose to walk with you

With you my heart can fear no more
 the hurt of selfish deeds
With you my body safely rests
 on steel gentility

Our steps may not fall as we choose
 or always synchronize
still we wander, parallel
 to where our future lies

Earthly riches come and go
 quickly cast aside
I care not for such frivolities
Just stroll with me in stride

Against the wind, on broken stone
 or beach awash with dew-
what rough or velvet path we tread
 I choose to walk with you.

Who else? For Eric, my one and only

XXI

Un jour avec mon petit chou
(a day with my little cabbage)

We sat in a café by an open window, inhaling the view,
 with red dahlia and yellow daisies splashing out of their box,
  all gazing upon the lively cobbled street.
While English tourists both engaged and repulsed the locals,
  the Quebecois went on about their business.

We ordered in French, it was easy for you,
  something with eggs, and cream, of course
taking our tea with a biscuit
    speckled with a zest
    we couldn't quite identify
 savoring every bite ~ and later for me, the moment
Chortling over our how we told a *petite* lie (are any really little?)
   to be out on our own,
  away from those who'd not relish our escapade.

Stepping into the happy frenzy, we set out to explore.

As if summoned, the elegantly aged, sturdy carriage pulled up beside us,
 the driver engaging us in flirty banter ~
and away we clopped with our new friends.

The knowledge, the passion he had for his culture and country!
 Touring *Vieux Quebec* with charming, witty Michel,
   such adorable Franglais!
And Piccolo in his Sunday best harness,
 looking as ancient as the city and majestic in his grandeur,
   obligingly smooth in his steps around traffic.

Michel graciously stopped at a souvenir store,
        helping us find our relics, our *bon marches*
*Quel beau souvenir** Michel would make, I whispered
        aah, but no...

Most precious, we took cuddly photos for our mementos~
    as if I needed one to remember.

And never stopped giggling whenever the memory arose.

*what a nice souvenir

The backstory: My Mumsy and I took a trip to Montreal to visit family, deciding during the stay to venture out to Quebec City, a 3 hour drive away. My grumpy Uncle Jacques was not in favor of the trip (he had an opinion for everything!), so we lied to him and said we were going elsewhere, shopping, somewhere girly, so he'd stop being a nuisance and feel unwelcome to join us. We made our escape down the Autoroute, acting as though we'd just pulled off a heist.

Mumsy and I visited St. Anne de Beaupre, an inspiring basilica where many infirmed people made pilgrimages, leaving behind their crutches, canes, even wheelchairs, all strapped floor to ceiling on enormous pillars framing the church entrance. We prayed and lit candles there, then drove along the scenic St. Lawrence Seaway. Later, we power walked the mammoth Chateau Frontenac, strolled and shopped around Old Quebec, capping off the day with a late, sumptuous bistro lunch followed by the frolicking carriage ride with Michel and his horse, Piccolo, the highlight of our 8 hour holiday.   (I was quite smitten with Michel, a dark eyed, pony-tailed Adonis, as he was with me.)

Upon returning to the car, we were shocked to find a flat tire. We both looked at it, then each other, exploding with weeping laughter, simultaneously joking that Jacques had arranged the hit, or God was punishing us for lying despite our devout church visit. A policeman happened by; I charmed him into changing the tire for me, hugged him a thank you, and off we zoomed back to Montreal – with a memory we hooted about for the rest of our life together.

Footnote: a French term of endearment, *mon petit chou* literally translates to "my little cabbage" but intentionally means "dear one". My great uncle Jean Dubuc dubbed Mumsy *"mon petit chou"*.

XXII

Holding hands

My friend rescues me
 no matter the cost
throughout all my trials,
  failures and loss
My friend marches with me
  And lifts me, renewed
A Jesus-sent angel,
  My friend is you.

For Kathy S.
May 5th 2013

XXIII

Ramblin' Rosebud

A face in the race,
  I'm a girly gambler
  betting my sweat on the finish line.
The training time, early hours,
 stroking long wet laps
 pushing up steep inclines
 stretching my strides
 is done.

Today's the day.
Swimmin' women
Biker chicks
runnin', ramblin'
 scramblin'

My gear is packed, my psyche filled
  with loving encouragement from friends
  (and my dearest love of all)

Now it's up to me
 to stroke faster,
  pump harder,
  tread further
with all the power I have
 testing this body
to its ultimate limits.

I offer a prayer
 not simply to finish,
(that is never enough)

 but to strive for excellence
knowing I have given my all,
 done right by my Creator
 using my gifts endowed me.

When it's over
I exhale. I laugh. I cry.
I know
I can do anything I am determined to do.

I earn a medal
that is mine forever
I am happy and proud.

The backstory: I trained 4 months for my first triathlon in which I competed on May 19th, 2013. Though it was a sprint or "baby" Tri – 225yard swim, 9mile bike, 2mile run – it took all I had to physically and emotionally prepare for this event. The best part? Ok, two best parts: first, it was a *women only* event, totally uplifting and buckets of fun. Second, I'm now hooked on Tri training and shopping for smaller sizes. Though I was blitzed by younger, fitter females, I placed 2nd in my age group : 60-64. I have a medal. I am truly happy and proud.

XXIV

DON'T SNUB ME

It ain't just pride
I'm justified
not satisfied
too long waitin'
 for equality
Don't you snub your nose at me
You think your skin is all I see?
No ma'am!
You get your food off my black back
I cut, clean and kindly pack
your chicken,
it don't grow like that.
I pick the beans
you almondine
I'm tired of waitin'
for the next Messiah
for my kingdom to come
for my luck to change
for a decent chance
for a life that matters.
I want the good life
just like you.
I aim to earn it
just like you.

Don't stand in my way
is all I ask
Don't make it harder
than it already is.

We all born with the same parts
Why's it that
the first thing broken
is the heart?

The backstory: In reading *The Warmth Of Other Suns*, I was enlightened as never before to the hardships survived, battles fought, lost, and won over the last 150 years by African Americans, our fellow citizens. I don't claim to be a history buff, but having read about, watched and experienced the '60's, I've borne witness to this humiliating and senseless societal chasm fueled by racism. Some say modest progress has been made, yet glaring economic disparities persist stemming from lopsided access to education, decent health care and employment opportunities. Beyond the efforts of my generation, I pray my children and their peers will be the engines of change in achieving true equality.

The poet Langston Hughes has long been a favorite of mine. I am captivated by his lyrical voice shining through each of his works, from prideful to tearful, a voice that resounds with a spine of tenacity and wisdom, a heart of hell fire and mercy, one who personifies the rugged souls among us, those who keep getting up and trying, giving the world a fresh chance, every day. His words, his voice gave birth to this piece and true enough, were simply my inspiration.

August 24th, 2013

XXV

RED'S EULOGY

When I was asked to do this for my brother, Bobby, I thought of the challenge in describing a life that matters. His sure did. It's hard to encapsulate someone's life in a few words, to paint a verbal picture of what that person meant to all of us gathered and to those who wanted to be here. Ultimately, it began to gel, recollections of fun times, teaching moments, hardships, generosity, and of course, his story telling and sense of humor. Experiences we shared with Bobby simply would not have been the same with anyone else. Most of all, friendship – Bobby was quick to adopt someone for whom he'd do just about anything he was asked.

During my time growing up and living here in RI, I remember Bobby attending numerous wakes and funerals for people, both close and distant, friends of friends, people to whom he purely wished to pay his respects . My family and I shook many hands at Bobby's wake, some faces were new to us. You were also Bobby's family: close friends he embraced and anointed as his own.

It's impossible to memorialize Bobby without including sports, whether as a participant or fan. He played basketball recreationally and ran track in high school. My earliest memory of him is racing down Hope St. onto Wickenden. Sports – that's where our lives began intersecting. We cheered for the Celts during the Red Auerbach dynasty and the Bruins during Bobby Orr's domination, informing each other the latest scores, stats and great plays. (The Boston Patriots didn't give us much to cheer about back then).

Bobby taught me how to fish and bait a hook. We used earthworms, sometimes clamworms, the kind with pincers. I found out years later that he had me do it because he hated worms, they were mushy and slimy and he didn't want to be pinched! This fear of goo extended to the beach. Bobby and I went to Galilee many times. Though he couldn't swim well, he loved the water – and hated seaweed. Naturally, I would scoop some up and fling it at him every chance I got just to watch him freak out.
It was very entertaining.

He got me back ten times over. When I started playing sandlot ball as a pre-teen, he took me aside, taught me to pitch, hold and swing a bat properly, field a ball and execute a hook slide. It is painful learning a hook slide, especially with a brother/coach whose main refrain was "try it again!"

Baseball. That was the titanic gift Bobby shared with me. He schooled me on how to play, read a box score, follow trades, and of course, who to love – the Red Sox. I came on board as a fan in 1967; we all remember that year (at least, those of us over 50). Bobby and I would sometimes listen to games together. Yes, listen, on the radio! Though the season ended just shy of winning the big one, it ordained us as Fenway Faithful and changed every fan's life forever, including ours. I still have the 1967 beer stein issued by the Narragansett Brewery that Bobby gave me celebrating the Sox as American League Champions. (One of his old jokes: what do you call a Portuguese Red Sox fan? Arruda!)

Our activities together expanded beyond Red Sox and PawSox games, including rides up to Boston to pick up his paychecks when he worked for the railroad. We'd often play cards and games, from our youth well into adulthood. Bobby taught me 500 and gin rummy as well as black jack, slap hockey and how to play chess – which I never took a shine to. When our Canadian family visited, they'd often play cards with Bobby into the wee hours; there was usually a LaBatt's or two involved.
Our French cousins always wanted to hang out with Bobby; he made himself available for their visits and routinely managed to have time off to spend with them. He'd take them down to Oakland Beach, Rocky Point, and Galilee for clam cakes and seafood. He got around quite a bit for a guy who had trouble with directions. Bobby may not have traveled the most direct route but he always found a way to get there.

When our cousin Jean Louis from Montreal was out of work, he moved in with us while Bobby facilitated local jobs for him. Bobby took Jean Louis around, introducing him to his social circuit. Typical Bobby – helping out someone and making it fun, all at once.

Around the time Bobby and Judy began dating, he'd moved into the 3rd floor of our Wickenden St tenement house. This coincided with his "friends of animals" period. Bobby had pigeons in the attic (one named Hector from Exeter), snapping turtles in the bathtub (I nearly lost a fingertip verifying this), along with rabbits, fish and canaries. We had our own little circle of life. One day, not knowing the pigeons were out of their cages, I unwittingly opened the attic door. They were as shocked as I was and began flapping furiously around the room, squawking and making a mess. I was screaming, they were molting and pooping all over me and the room, it was straight out of Hitchcock. With that, our mom reached her limit and finally got him to break up the zoo and air out the rooms. Bobby began adopting more standard pets like kittens and puppies.

We had a pool table in that apartment – which he somehow hauled up 2 flights of narrow, winding steps to the 3rd floor, no doubt with the help of husky pals. The pool room became a central gathering place for our family and friends. Bobby taught the game to me and a few girlfriends; by the time we were 13, my girlie gang and I knew how to shoot combos, bank shots and use topspin. We were wicked cool! He won more than a few bets shooting pool in local hangouts. You had to watch out for him. We also used the table for ping pong and launched many balls out that 3rd floor window - then hung out over the gutter, watching people's traumatized reactions to floating projectiles over Wickenden St.

Apart from our ancient Italian neighbors growing grapes for table wine, Bobby was the first male gardener I ever knew. Wherever he lived, he grew a variety of vegetables; he faithfully watched Victory Garden and fawned over his Big Boy tomatoes to insure their success.

It's amazing to me now that, in spite of being 10 years older, Bobby shared such an enormous chunk of his time with me, his kid sister. We even had special names for each other. I named him Red, for Red Rolfe, a former Yankees 3rd baseman with whom he became fixated upon reading Rolfe's obit. He dubbed me Little Iodine, a comic strip character whose job it was to be the family pest. I did my best to live up to that. Of course, there came a time I wasn't so fond of his attention – when I began dating. For much longer than I desired, Bobby screened prospective boyfriends, putting them on notice: he was watching them. He was my gatekeeper.

When I lose someone I've loved, I often wish I had done things differently. I think it's pretty human for most of us, wishing we had spent more time together or had a chance to hit the reset button. Lamenting is predictable but not constructive, doesn't help us cope and move on from heartache. I've agonized over losing people close to me, close enough that I've cried over losing them and longed to have them back.

Bobby, of course, was chief among them. Over time, a lesson evolved: I do have a God given opportunity to do things better and differently right now. We don't get a mulligan with someone we've lost, but we do get a fresh chance every day, with each sunrise, to give and be our best with everyone here in our lives at this moment.
Bobby's prime characteristics, the things we loved most about him, were his fun spirit, sense of humor, good heart, his sociability, his friendliness. Going forward, let that be Bobby's gift and inspiration to us. Let kindness prevail in every word and deed, and like Bobby, may we all live a life that matters.

Eileen Anderson, Raleigh NC, August 2013

The backstory: My brother Bobby died August 1st, 2013. We hadn't been close for a while. Suffice to say I agonized over that and wished I'd tried harder to catch one more game with him. In loss, we gain lessons and perspective. Time is precious, as are the people we treasure. Relationships evaporate unless we make time for them. I wouldn't be the baseball lover and Red Sox fan I am today without Bobby's guidance and influence. Though his departure was not what I ever envisioned, I give thanks that I was lucky enough to be Bobby's sister.

Footnote: I never publicly offered this eulogy. Bobby's funeral was arranged quickly and without a church service where I would have proudly honored him.

XXVI

Poppa's Song

I am your dad
      the man in your life
who, with your beautiful mother,
      my wife
once had a dream
      to cherish a child
and though we had to
      wait for a while
we counted the days,
      me and your mom
now here you are nestled
      all snug in my arms.
Through every growth spurt,
      heartbreak, and craze
I am your shelter
      in good or bad days.
But right now, this moment,
      exquisite sweet treasure
know that for always
      you are loved beyond measure.

Celebrating the birth of Jamie, Sept 12th, 2014 at 7:41am

www.ingramcontent.com/pod-product-compliance
Lightning Source LLC
Chambersburg PA
CBHW071315200626
46813CB00015B/2221